The Bear Necessities
of Grief

written and illustrated by
Duane S. Montague

ISBN: 9781790987139

DEDICATION

This book is dedicated to my grandmother,
Margret Woodhouse.

More than twenty years after she began the journey
modeled in this book, she had shown thousands of people
that death is not the end, that the parting of my grandfather
was just the beginning of a new life.

When she passed away at 96, her memorial service
was packed with hundreds of people who had never known
her before my grandfather passed away.

Her journey shows us that grief may be a
journey you don't choose to take, but how you respond
can not only change your life, but leave
a huge impact on the lives of others.

SPECIAL THANKS

Thank you to my wife, Robyn, for her support and love as we have journeyed through grief together several times since this book was originally written.

We have walked this road more than we could have imagined, and through it we have grown closer as a family and learned to enjoy so many more of the moments life sends our way.

ACKNOWLEDGEMENTS

Thank you especially to the many readers, counselors, and grief recovery groups who have found me online, across the years, to ask me for more copies of this book.
I am grateful for your support,
and so thankful for the impact my little book
has had on so many people over the years.

ABOUT THIS BOOK

It's best to read this book through once,
perhaps when you first start your journey.
There are 30 readings and illustrations to help guide your
thoughts, encourage your heart, and lift your spirit—
but some may not "fit" where you currently are.

That's okay.

This journey is unique to you.
While many people may experience it, and some may even
join you along the way, there is no "right way."
There is only one way—your personal road.

Wishing you peace, hope, and yes, *joy* in the journey.

INTRODUCTION

Until my Grandpa Woodhouse passed away in 1997, I had honestly never truly experienced grief. I remember being sad about our different pets dying over the years, but until that dark night when I sang "I'll Be Seeing You" to him and said goodbye for the last time, I didn't understand the heart-wrenching, constant aching, un-ending emotional pain of grief.

This book was written in response to the journey our family started that day, one of loss and pain, but steeped still in hope and the promises we had believed—and he had preached—all his life. While it was incredibly difficult to say goodbye to this beloved man, we didn't mourn without purpose, and our grief became part of the solace that came with knowing our parting was not forever.

I don't know what pain you're feeling today, or what loss you have encountered. I do know that it will not last forever, and even though you did not choose to start the journey you are on today, if you walk it slowly and carefully, you *will* reach the end of the road. You will discover much about yourself along the way, and you will have many opportunities to grow, to find hope, and to stay connected and close to the one you have lost.

Jesus told her, "I am the resurrection and the life.
Anyone who believes in me will live, even after dying."
(John 11:25, NLT

1.

You have begun a journey you did not choose to take. While this new road will take you many places, some unfamiliar and frightening, remember that you are not alone.

2.

You will experience pain and loss, memories and "what-might-have-beens." Go through each of these feelings and emotions—don't be afraid of them. There is really no way out of grief, there is only a way through it.

3.

Don't be afraid to ask, "Why?" You cannot see the reasons, and you may not find the answers, but the question will help ease the pain in your soul.

4.

Don't be afraid to hurt. Your pain is real and will not be ignored, no matter how hard you may try. This hurt is only another way of showing your love for the one you have lost.

5.

Find solace in the company of others who share your loss. Your bond with them is more than familial, more than friendship. Grief is a spiritual bond between people who have experienced what it truly means to be human.

6.

Sometimes you may need to cast blame. Doctors, medication, even God—you may feel the need to blame someone for the emptiness you are feeling.

That's okay.

There's nothing wrong with these feelings. Just remember that where you are right now is not the final destination on your journey.

7.

Guilt may overwhelm you. Guilt for things you forgot to do—and for things you did. You may even feel guilt because you are still alive. Remember, grief is not about what happened, nor what is happening.

It is about where you are going to be.

8.

Remember, you are now a different person. You will never be the same, even though glimpses of the old you may surface once in a while. Don't be afraid of the new person you are becoming.

9.

You will now look at life differently.

Your loss will cast a new light on everything you do, the places you go, the people you talk with. Don't be afraid of the new life you are living.

10.

At times you will feel very alone.
Surrounded by people who care, you
may suddenly feel a heartache so great
that you are overwhelmed by it. In those
moments, step away from people, and
try to draw closer to God. He is the only
source of comfort for the soul.

11.

Cherish the memory of your loved one by telling stories about him, by displaying pictures of her. As you laugh and cry about your time together, you will be reminded of the connection you will always share.

12.

The connection between you and your loved one will sometimes be marked by a hollow emptiness that nothing can fill. Leave it alone. Cherish that empty space because it is the part of you still occupied by your loved one.

13.

Be honest when people ask how you are doing. Don't disguise your pain—being dishonest about your hurt will only deepen it. If you are not "All right," don't pretend that you are. It is okay to tell the truth about your grief.

14.

There will be times when you are angry at God. Express your anger, your frustration, your hurt, your questions, and regrets. Remember that His love is great enough to hold your pain and anger until you are able to carry it for yourself again.

15.

Well-meaning friends may say things that wound your spirit. You may be very aware that "It was God's will" or "It is probably better this way," but it doesn't make hearing others say it any easier. Turn these words over to God—His grace can help you see beyond the hurt they caused to the love that was intended.

16.

Wrist-watch time is not God's time.
Though we may measure years with
clocks and calendars, God does not.

When you look at life through His eyes,
you see that all times are *now*. The good
times you had in the past can be yours
again, today.

You just need to live in God's time—not
your own.

17.

Find joy in the midst of your grief. It may seem hidden, but joy is still available to you: in the laughter of friends, the smile of a child, the memory of time spent with your loved one. Joy can still be yours—you may just need to look for it.

18.

Find peace in the midst of your grief. It may seem impossible, when your soul is in turmoil and sleep is hard to come by, but peace can be found in the middle of even the worst of life's storms. Look for places to be quiet and moments to be still, and you will find rest.

19.

Find forgiveness in the midst of your grief. It may seem difficult, and nearly impossible right now, but until you can forgive—God, doctors, even yourself— you will never be able to complete the journey through grief.

20.

Get some rest.
Get as much as you can.

While sleep may be difficult, take time to be quiet and calm. Don't keep yourself busy—this will only distract you from the journey and make it even longer.

21.

Decide how you will deal with the next step in your journey. You know you will never be the same, but what kind of future will you have?

Will you stay rooted in the past because that is where your loved one was? Or will you move into a future where hope and joy are possible because that is what lies ahead of you?

22.

Sometimes your sense of loss will overwhelm you. You may wonder how you can ever bear the burden you have shouldered. Remember that you are not alone.

Your journey is unique to you, but you have loved ones who will gladly be there to help when your grief is too much to carry alone.

23.

When your loved one died, you lost a part of yourself that can never be recovered. But what will you gain as you continue your journey? Be prepared to grow, to be challenged. There is still much for you to learn.

24.

Seek out the company of others who have also experienced grief. But make sure they are people who focus on tomorrow, not yesterday, who live with hope, not regret. When you walk together through the hard times and dark moments, these fellow travelers will help light your way.

25.

On days that were important to you and your loved one, celebrate! Celebrate the life they lived and the life you are living. Don't avoid birthdays, holidays, or anniversaries because of the past—use them as a launching point for creating new, wonderful memories.

26.

Are there things you needed to say to your loved one, and never had the chance? It's not too late. Write letters to him, talk often to her. Though the response may be unheard, you will feel it in your heart and know that you will be okay.

27.

As your journey continues, you will find the pain lessening. Don't be afraid of it. You are not betraying your loved one. You are simply trading regret and sorrow for hope and joy, despair and loss for peace and comfort.

28.

Someday, when you are far from where you started, you will look back at the journey you have taken. You will see the long and winding road you have walked. And you will realize that in spite of all you have faced, you have come a very long way.

29.

Think of your journey as one that started in the dark of night. In that dim light, you began your travels, afraid and uncertain—aware only of the emptiness surrounding you.

But day follows night, and what seemed so impossible at first has become a path filled with unexpected moments of rest and peace—and you can at last see farther than ever before.

30.

Grief will bring you in contact with the deepest human fears and emotions. It will also challenge you to go beyond your human understanding, to find peace in the midst of the storm, to find joy in the depths of sorrow. In the end, you will have brushed eternity—*and be forever changed.*

AFTERWORD

I wrote this book in 1999. My grandfather passed away shortly before Easter two years earlier, and it was the first death I felt deeply. He and I were close and kindred spirits, sharing a love for music and mischief, and his death left a giant hole in my heart.

My grandmother was married to him for 56 years, and they had traveled the world, ministered across the United States, and pastored churches throughout Washington state when he died. She could have turned inward and decided her life ended when his did.

I ended up living with her for nearly two years after he passed away. Being the only single member of the family, I was the logical choice to be the one to move in and keep her from being alone, and we already shared an affinity for murder mysteries and British television.

I got to watch firsthand as she walked the journey described in this book. It was not her first time—she'd lost her parents and at least two sisters at this point in her life—

but this was different, because it was the man who had shared most of her life.

She and I would talk often about Grandpa and she would share her thoughts on how she was dealing with his loss, and ask me how I was doing as well. Many of the thoughts shared her were part of our honest and heartfelt conversations over those years, often over dinner as we talked and laughed and cried.

We continued to celebrate his birthday every year, releasing balloons into the sky at Red Robin—just like we had that final birthday we had shared with him. We kept his picture featured in prominent places throughout our apartment, and the jazz music he loved played frequently on the small stereo she kept in her bedroom. Even after I met my future wife and started bringing her home to hang out, Grandma would eat with us and laugh with us, and Robyn got to know the grandfather I loved so much through her.

Grief is a journey nobody wishes to take. It's not something we would wish on anyone, either. But when we walk this unexpected journey, something happens. It sounds cliché, but it's true: you don't end the same person you were when you began it. You either change for the better or worse, and that choice is entirely up to you.

My grandmother passed away at the age of 96,

nearly 20 years after my grandpa died. In that 20 years, she grew and changed, and the person she was when she died was not the same woman I had known as a child.

When I was a boy, my grandfather had been the fun and impulsive one, usually smiling, and always encouraging. My grandmother was the strict disciplinarian, reminding us to wash our faces in the morning, and holding both my grandpa and us accountable when too many cookies went missing.

My grandmother spent the next 20 years being the fun and caring, always encouraging and entertaining woman she hadn't been able to be when living with Grandpa. With him gone, she chose to be the one to hide chocolate in her closet for the great-grandkids to find, to take them out on adventures from miniature golf to high tea, and to remind their parents to enjoy life more.

She could have said, "I've done my time serving," but in 2001 she took her first lead in a stage musical I'd created, acted frequently in other shows, and began volunteering at the local clinic to help old people who were much younger than her. She continued to share her faith and deepen friendships and although she could be irascible, even those who disagreed with her politics found her charming.

Her journey through grief freed her to become an even better version of herself. She still communicated with my grandfather, writing him long letters on her Mac every evening. She wrote out her life story to share with her family, and left us with a long written record of the adventures she shared with him for more than 50 years.

Watching her walk through grief helped when my other grandparents passed away in the subsequent years. Her understanding of the pain of loss was a huge gift to Robyn when her mother passed away just a decade into our marriage. She helped us realize the importance of keeping memories alive, of sharing stories, and refusing to give in to despair or sadness or the defeat that death seems to imply.

I do not believe that death is the end. I do believe in eternity and in heaven and in a God who loves us and created each of us for life with each other and with Him. My grandparents believed this, and as a pastor who has performed many funeral and memorial services over the years, I must admit that I believe it, too.

My hope for you is that you will be encouraged to find hope in the midst of the brokenness of grief. I hope you discover joy in the middle of your sorrow. It's my prayer that this book will encourage you to look for something more and bigger than yourself as you take this journey, and that you will be surprised by what you discover.

Ultimately, though, my wish for you is that you may discover what my grandmother discovered: this journey may not be the one you chose, but if you walk it carefully and purposefully, it will enable you to not only live your life with a greater purpose—it will help you leave the world a much better place.

ABOUT THE AUTHOR

Duane S. Montague is the author of *Resting Merry: Discovering Joy and Peace at Christmas, Let Go,* and the author/illustrator of the nine books in the *Bear Necessities* series. In addition, he is a featured writer for David C. Cook's *The Action Bible* and *The Action Bible Devotional,* creator of more than 20 stage musicals and hundreds of live stage shows. He is a teaching pastor at Journey Church and featured speaker at national conferences and workshops.

He is married to Robyn, has four kids and two cats, and lives in Southern California, where he enjoys the sunshine, proximity to Disneyland, and finding joy through road trips across the United States.

You can find him online at duanesm.com, on Facebook, and on Instagram.

The Bear Necessities of Acceptance
The Bear Necessities of Caring for Yourself
The Bear Necessities for Families
The Bear Necessities of Friendship
The Bear Necessities of Grief
The Bear Necessities of Happiness
The Bear Necessities of Life
The Bear Necessities of Love
The Bear Necessities of Simplicity

Made in the USA
Las Vegas, NV
15 June 2021